Michael Jacobs

Getting Along Famously

BROADWAY PLAY PUBLISHING INC
New York
www.broadwayplaypublishing.com
info@broadwayplaypublishing.com

GETTING ALONG FAMOUSLY

Copyright 1981 and 1986 by Michael Jacobs

All rights reserved. This work is fully protected under the copyright laws of the United States of America.

No part of this publication may be photocopied, reproduced, stored in a retrieval system, or transmitted, in any form or by any means, electronic, mechanical, recording, or otherwise, without the prior permission of the publisher. Additional copies of this play are available from the publisher.

Written permission is required for live performance of any sort. This includes readings, cuttings, scenes, and excerpts. For amateur and stock performances, please contact Broadway Play Publishing, Inc.

For all other rights, please contact Rosenstone/Wender, 3 East 48th Street, New York, New York 10017.

First printing: August 1986
ISBN: 978-0-88145-038-5

Design by Marie Donovan
Set in Baskerville by L&F Technical Composition, Lakeland, FL
Printed and bound by Cushing-Malloy, Ann Arbor, MI

For my mother
who read to me

HUDSON GUILD THEATRE

DAVID KERRY HEEFNER Producing Director

DANIEL SWEE Associate Director

presents

GETTING ALONG FAMOUSLY

by

MICHAEL JACOBS

Directed by
JOAN DARLING

with

TOM ALDREDGE*	**TED FLICKER***
BEVERLY NERO*	**EDWARD POWER***

Set Design by **JAMES LEONARD JOY**   *Costume Design by* **MARIANN VERHEYEN**   *Lighting Design by* **PHIL MONAT**

Production Stage Manager
BRIAN KAUFMAN*

January 25 — February 19, 1984

This event is made possible in part with public funds from the New York State Council on the Arts and the National Endowment for the Arts.

*Members of Actor's Equity Association

CAST
(in order of appearance)

Harry Leeby .... TED FLICKER
Lori Leeby .... BEVERLY NERO
Sandy Castle .... TOM ALDREDGE
Justin Dean .... EDWARD POWER

The Time: The Present

The Place: New York City. The brownstone mansion of Harry Leeby. His study.

THERE WILL BE ONE FIFTEEN-MINUTE INTERMISSION.

Act One

Scene One

(*New York City — the brownstone mansion of* HARRY LEEBY; *his study.*)

(*There are indications of vast wealth here. The woods are oak and mahogany, the carpet is deep pile, and the sofa is plush and inviting. The room features an extensive library, shelving running floor to ceiling, wall to wall, containing books of various sizes, hardcover, softcover, and leatherbound. There is a library ladder for access to the higher shelves.* HARRY'S *desk is antique, polished, and grand. Right of the desk is an extension upon which sits a beaten-up manual typewriter and bookends supporting the sixteen novels* HARRY *has written as Ducan Foster. Indeed,* HARRY *is the pen behind Axel Troy.*)

(*At rise*)

(*Books.* HARRY LEEBY/*Duncan Foster is fifty-one years old. He sits at his desk amid several piles of books, as well as single books turned to particular passages. He wears silk pajamas under a velvet robe which belies his manner of flannel and terrycloth. The room is dark, window curtains drawn, a small desk lamp offering the only light, and quiet, except for the clock ticking.*)

HARRY: (*Reads aloud*) The Adventures of Huckleberry Finn. Chapter One.

(*The telephone rings.* HARRY *lifts the receiver from the cradle and lays it on the desk.*)

RECEIVER: (*The voice of* SANDY CASTLE) Harry! Four million dollars! Half a million the hardcover, two million against twenty percent of the motion picture plus whatever I scribbled here about recoupment. Oh, you know what you get when the movie makes its money back? I can't read this but it's terrific! Let it be a surprise.

HARRY: (*Continues aloud*) You don't know about me without you have read a book by the name of *The Adventures of Tom Sawyer*; but that ain't no matter. That book was made by Mr. Mark Twain, and he told the truth, mainly.

RECEIVER: Overseas options; I have in front of me, the world! And every little country has a big number on it. We got Europe, Scandinavia, Australia, Pakistan, they love you in Karachi, Harry! Let me just give this a quick spin and see if I missed anywhere. What's this other million and a half, here?

HARRY: (*Another book*) Old Marley was as dead as a door-nail.

RECEIVER: Paperback! Ahh! I spilled the coffee. All the zeroes are running down the page!

HARRY: (*Continues aloud*) This must be distinctly understood or nothing wonderful can come of the story I am going to relate.

RECEIVER: All right, forget it. Their legal's calling your legal. We all want to put our names on this and get lunch so tell Garfield easy on the clauses. He starts with his clauses, nobody eats. You know what? Forget Garfield. I got you a perfectly good arrangement. Whereas; they print the book and make the movie and you get whatever you want. I think those are equitable terms and advise you to sign.

HARRY: (*Continuing aloud*) I see a vacant seat, replied the Ghost, in the poor chimney corner, and a crutch without an owner, carefully preserved. If these shadows remain unaltered by the future, the child will die.

RECEIVER: Harry! Why aren't you talking to me? Don't you like your four million?

HARRY: (*Continues aloud*) And so, as Tiny Tim observed, God bless Us, Every One!

(*He closes the book and lays his head on the desk.*)

RECEIVER: Because my ten percent is four hundred thousand and I like my . . . (*Wildly*) . . . four hundred thousand dollars! Harry! Let me make this deal! Let me scratch out a living.

HARRY: (*His head next to the receiver*) Maybe not a great novel. Maybe not a classic piece of literature because even now I have a representative sampling piled on my desk and in going through them I know they each contain something rare and individual I may not contain in me, I admit it you hear me? But one good book.

Act One

RECEIVER: You want me to call them back and turn it down? Fine. You're right. I'll ask four and a half. It's worth four and a half if it's worth a penny! (*With some trepidation*) Four and a half, geez Harry, you sure?

HARRY: I love a good book.

(*He reaches out a hand and shuts off the lamp. The room is dark.*)

RECEIVER: Fine. You're right. I'm calling now. I'm putting you on hold. I know nobody's ever done that to you before, it's where I go away and come back. You don't have to do anything.

(*The receiver clicks. HARRY is on hold.*)

(LORI LEEBY *enters. She is* HARRY'S *daughter, assistant, and link to the outside world. She is twenty-four years old, wears a running suit, and carries a tray of coffee and muffins, and a manuscript.*)

LORI: You slept in here again.

(*She sets the tray on the desk and places the manuscript in front of her father.*)

HARRY: You read it?

(*She pulls the window curtains open. Sunlight floods the room.*)

LORI: At least let me bring a bed in here.

HARRY: I slept on the floor. (*Takes one of the books in front of him, finds a place, and reads.*) Charles Dickens was born on February 7th, 1812, Portsmouth, England, the son of improvidence. As a youngster he knew hunger, deprivation, child labor, and debtor's prison. (*Takes one of his own books from the bookends, finds a place, and reads.*) Duncan Foster was born on May 25th, 1931, Great Neck, New York, the son of an orthodontist. He wrote his first Axel Troy novel at twenty-six and was instantly famous. (*He sighs.*)

LORI: (*Offers*) Here. You'll feel better with this muffin in you.

HARRY: No. People on the West Side are starving.

(*The receiver clicks on.*)

RECEIVER: Harry! Four and a half million! They didn't even blink.

(HARRY *hangs up the phone and stares at it.*)

HARRY: I ignore him, he thinks I'm unhappy with the deal he made so he makes a better one and doesn't understand why I never take his calls. (*Turns*) Lori.

LORI: Yes. I read it.

HARRY: Oh.

(*They look at each other.*)

LORI: Axel finally has his way with Mademoiselle Yvette Bonsoir.

HARRY: I figure I owed him as much.

LORI: After all of their chance rendezvous. On the slopes at Gstaad, on the beach at Capri, something always managed to keep them from each other at that last moment. But now he has her! And right in his own backyard. New York City. (*Looking out the window.*) Eighty-first Street. (*A bit let down*) In the back of a taxicab.

HARRY: Mademoiselle Yvette Bonsoir, after sixteen hardcovers, paperbacks, feature films, movies of the week and late shows, breaks down trembling, takes his hand longingly into her own, places it gently upon her qivering breast, and, breathing tremulously into his ear, admits her lusting, insatiate desire. (*Shrugs*) They happen to be in traffic. (LORI *picks up the manuscript, turn to the last page, and reads.*)

LORI: . . . As Axel found ten-cent heaven with each ninth of a mile, he never noticed the three Checkers glide up and catch them at the light. The upper cushions of the back seat slid open and Bonsoir rolled herself away from him, into the trunk. "C'est fini, mon amour" she whispered, and gave up one crystalline tear. It splashed on Axel's parted lips but he never felt the drop. It took a baker's dozen of the KGB elite. The sub machine gun rattled salutations and the stilettos whistled a more personal tune, this, to be their song eternally, as Bonsoir legged it down Lexington Avenue and revolved herself into Bloomingdale's. Axel sensed no interruption. His dreams were dizzy and his head danced a snappy tango, rushing his blood into the open like roses in unwilling bloom. Time pulsed fancy colors. Swirling reds turned flowing purple and

Act One

drained away to black surrender. He figured he was dead. No broad was that good. The end.

(*She looks at her father. The telephone rings.* HARRY *grabs it.*)

HARRY: (*Into the phone*) Sandy, it's the middle of the day, what kind of time is this to call me? (*Deflated*) Oh, hello Justin. (*He leans against his desk and rubs his chest.*) Do we just have a good connection or are you somewhere in the area, Heaven forfend. LaGuardia? Why? (*Rubs harder*) Okay, I know why. Yeah, Sandy sold it. I don't know for how much, it depends how long I can avoid him. You'll be fine in this one, you'll do just like you've done in all of the others. (*He clutches at his chest.*) No, I don't understand why the Academy ignores you. They just don't give Oscars to spies. I know you're a legend, it's not you, it's the genre. No, I don't know the requirements for the Jean Hirscholt Humanitarian Award.

LORI: Why couldn't he just have been shot once neatly through the heart?

HARRY: (*Into the phone*) Of course I understand the ending Justin, I wrote it!

(LORI *returns the books on her father's desk to their proper shelves.*)

HARRY: (*Into the phone*) Yeah, you can come over but my mind's made up Justin I'm hanging up on you. I know nobody's ever done that to you before, it's where I go away and never come back.

(*He hangs up. On the desk is a stand-up model gun, pointing at him. He pulls the trigger twice. It shoots two aspirins at him. He swallows them down with his coffee.*)

HARRY: Twenty-five years ago, on my knees, I begged them to get Paul Newman. They said, Justin Dean. I said, Steve McQueen. They said, Justin Dean. I said, Moe, Larry, Curly, Shemp, now he's coming over. How do I recognize him out of his tuxedo?

LORI: He's just swanky.

HARRY: Axel's not supposed to be swanky!

LORI: I like his accent.

HARRY: Axel's not supposed to have an accent! And neither is Justin, since he was born in Brooklyn.

LORI: Justin's from London.

HARRY: Flatbush Avenue! And Justin is Norman. (*With glee*) I looked up his birth records.

LORI: Norman?

HARRY: Frumpkin. Shh! We're probably the only ones who know. I'm sure he's long forgotten.

LORI: Well, whoever he is, his audience loves him. And I can certainly understand him flying across the country to see you. Axel Troy is his whole life. Made him famous. Made you famous.

HARRY: Made Duncan Foster famous. Smothered Harry Leeby, like he smothered Norman Frumpkin, who's a terrific guy.

LORI: You don't like Justin.

HARRY: Hate him. But I'm figuring Norman for all right.

(*The telephone rings.* HARRY *lifts the receiver and holds it up.*)

RECEIVER: Four million, seven hundred and fifty thousand dollars!

(HARRY *hangs up the phone.*)

LORI: And what is that? I don't understand Sandy at all. He's been handling this like it was simply your next manuscript. Like he doesn't know what goes on, here. Like he hasn't even . . . (*She looks at her father incredulously.*) . . . read it!

HARRY: The last book Sandy read was *My Gun Is My Jury*.

LORI: Your first one.

HARRY: Ever since then he figures they're all the same and waits for the movie.

LORI: But the publisher . . . the studio . . .

HARRY: Reads. Mmn. For this one they really would give me whatever I want.

LORI: And you're not going to tell him?

HARRY: (*Shrugs*) There's nothing I want they can give me.

ACT ONE 7

(LORI *goes to the typewriter in the box.*)

LORI: Are you going to use this thing ever? Because the warranty's expired and the model's discontinued.

HARRY: Soon. Any day.

LORI: The longer it stays in here, the longer the world is deprived of your masterpiece. And the world is awaiting.

HARRY: What makes you think so?

LORI: (*Picks up one of* HARRY's *books.*) . . . With *My Gun Is My Jury, Sniper,* and *Gunshy,* Mr. Foster established himself as one of the most popular authors in a world always awaiting his next book.

HARRY: (*To his manual typewriter, which* LORI *has handed him.*) I tried for something different from this one but all it knows is bullets. I would type; Catrina knelt by the dying fire, memories of Fernando dancing in her soul . . . and it would type; . . . until her images were snuffed by the sickening thud of a thirty eight, crushing her skull . . . That's all it wants to do!

(*The doorbell rings.*)

HARRY: There's Justin, come to meet his Maker.

LORI: No. That's Stephen. We're running around the reservoir. And lunch in the park.

HARRY: (*Accusing*) You like this guy.

LORI: Uh huh.

HARRY: More than me?

LORI: (*Smiles*) Not yet. (*She exits.*)

(HARRY *sits at his electric typewriter and reads to it.*)

HARRY: . . . With *Oliver Twist, Nicholas Nickleby,* and *A Christmas Carol,* Mr. Dickens established himself as one of the most popular authors in a world always awaiting his next book. (*Sighs*) Dickens' exhausting workload contributed to his marriage ending in separation. (*Stops*) Ah. Common ground. We'd have had something to talk about, me and Charles. Charley. Chuck. (*Holds the book up to* the typewriter.) *David Copperfield*. By my buddy, Chuck Dickens. (*Reads*) Chapter One. I am born. Whether I shall turn out to be the hero of my own life, or whether that station will be held by anybody else, these pages must show. (*To the typewriter*) This is the sort of thing we'll be doing around here, now. Are you up to it? Yes and we're immortal, no and we die on the discount rack, a grizzly death and terrible humiliation, cover torn and naked dedication exposed to the passers by. (*He gestures toward his books.*) Look. Wisdom and style and we're going to add to it. (*Confidentially to the typewriter*) Don't be humiliated. You've got every letter right here. The complete works.

(*He switches it on. It jumps to life with a snap and a hum. He types something rapid fire and stops, pleased.*)

HARRY: Classic.

(LORI *enters.*)

LORI: It's not Stephen.

HARRY: Oh no.

LORI: It's not Justin, either.

HARRY: Oh no!

(*Finding no way out, he drops behind the desk as* SANDY CASTLE *bursts into the room. He is* HARRY'S *closest friend and literary representation. His clothes are tailored and expensive. He is manicured and holding a half-eaten, overstuffed sandwich. He is in his early fifties and presently a madman.*)

SANDY: I'm not a busy man! I've got time to go visiting! You drag me from my office from Times Square from the cutthroats and bloodsuckers all the way up to this wasteland where I'm uncomfortable out of my element, traffic's clogged up, somebody's famous everybody's looking six blocks away, I had to jump out of my cab and walk because you don't want to take my calls? Fine! Call me. I'm not in for you, anymore. Call me now. I'm not in. (*Looks around the room.*) Where are you?

HARRY: (*A voice behind the desk*) I'll give you five dollars to go away.

ACT ONE

SANDY: (*Moves to the desk and bends over it.*) Just don't get so big for your bathrobe, Harry. You can't buy me, I'm in your league, remember? I make what you make less ninety percent. (*Notices the paper in the typewriter.*) What's this, you're working?

HARRY: (*Pops up*) No. That's not anything.

(*He tries to pull it from the machine but* SANDY *grabs it first.*)

SANDY: (*Delighted*) You're working! Of course you can't be bothered. You know the creative flow is something for which I have only the greatest respect. (*He rests his sandwich on the typewriter.*) So, what do we have? (*Reads*) Now is the time for all good men to come to the aid of their country. (*Looks at* LORI.) This has been done.

HARRY: Lori. Honey. Don't you think it might be a good idea if you left us alone?

LORI: No. Bad idea. I can't miss this moment. My memoirs hinge on it.

SANDY: She's not going anywhere until she gives her Uncle Sandy a hug.

HARRY: He's not really your uncle, you don't have to.

SANDY: I held her while you changed her diapers, I'm entitled to hold her now that she's gorgeous. (*Hugs her*) Where're you going today, Gorgeous?

LORI: The park.

SANDY: The park. You young people. You don't realize the value of your youth, right Harry? (*To* LORI, *sagely*) I would give every cent I had to be your age and wealthy.

LORI: Come here.

(*She pulls* SANDY *to the desk and drapes his arm around her father's shoulder as she moves to the door.*)

LORI: Smile for me.

(*They smile for her.*)

LORI: Good. That's how I'm going to remember you.

(LORI *exits*. SANDY *looks at* HARRY.)

HARRY: Sandy, this is very difficult. I want you to listen and not say a word.

SANDY: Do you know how much it means to you to have me working for you?

HARRY: Forget business. This has nothing to do with business.

SANDY: Of course not. What do you want to know about business? All you want to know is tap, tap, tap.

HARRY: (*Picks up the manuscript.*) There's something about this you have to understand.

SANDY: (*Grabs it from him.*) Five million dollars! (*He slams it onto the desk.*) One half hour I'm explaining why this is worth five up front when we all know nothing's worth five up front, down front, in out, up back, thirty minutes I don't let them open their mouth because I'm afraid they're going to laugh in my face. You know what they say to five up front?

HARRY: They say good.

SANDY: They say good! I laughed in their face. Time and time again I amaze myself with my mastery of this business. (*He takes papers from his jacket pocket.*) Sign.

HARRY: Sandy, we have to talk.

SANDY: No talking. You're a writer. Write. (*Forces a pen on him.*) Write while they're out of their mind!

HARRY: Has Garfield seen this?

SANDY: Will you forget Garfield? He's a lawyer. He's going to find something wrong with it. Who wants that? (*Smiles*) Besides, he's already been through this already.

HARRY: How?

SANDY: (*Jubilant*) Because these are the same contracts as last time! Hah! I made copies. I just put a five million where the three million was and I saved you Garfield's fee, the yegg. Harry! Harr. We've been friends a good long time now and done very well for it. I am asking you to do something for your friend now. I am asking you to trust your friend and sign your name.

HARRY: Not before I tell you something.

SANDY: I'm asking for trust. There's nothing to tell.

HARRY: Not before I tell you.

SANDY: I'm asking for trust.

HARRY: Not before I . . .

SANDY: I'm asking.

HARRY: Not before . . .

SANDY: I'm asking.

HARRY: Not . . .

SANDY: Asking.

(*Pause*)

HARRY: (*Explodes*) Sandy!

SANDY: (*Explodes more*) Harry! You're as crazy as they are! (*Suddenly comforting*) It's okay. Shh. I'm here, kiddo. I'm right here. Not your fault. Crazy times we live in. Shh. Everybody's crazy.

(*He moves around the desk, puts the pen in* HARRY's *fingers and stands over him, guiding his hand into writing his name on the contract.*)

SANDY: See? This is how we write our name.

HARRY: This is not what you want.

SANDY: I know. Money, glory, boo, bad, shh, I'm here.

(*He gently takes the signed contract from* HARRY *and looks at it, moving away. He is completely lost in it and oblivious to everything else.*)

HARRY: Axel's gone.

SANDY: I'm rich.

HARRY: He's dead. I killed him.

SANDY: I'm a very rich boy.

HARRY: Now you know.

SANDY: I was rich, now I'm richer.

HARRY: I feel so much better.

SANDY: It's a wonderful life.

HARRY: Are you listening to me?

SANDY: Best of all I made Garfield obsolete. I'm ashamed of myself for not figuring this out fifteen deals ago.

HARRY: Because I have too much guilt about too many things not to make sure you're advised and aware.

(SANDY *picks up the phone and dials.*)

SANDY: I mean, this constitutes a . . . what's he get for drawing up your contracts, lately? Fifty, sixty grand? Significant loss. Too bad. I was always the clever one and he's a big boy, now. (*Into the phone*) Gloria? Give me Garfield.

HARRY: I'm guilty about my summer house on my island.

SANDY: (*Covers the phone*) Seven law diplomas hung on his walls in cheap wood frames from so-so schools didn't make him. I made him. And I didn't need to. All I needed was a quarter for the copy machine.

HARRY: I never visit my mountain anymore.

SANDY: I can't wait to break this to him tactfully.

HARRY: And it's not the guilt that's abnormal, Sandy, because it's grown too perfectly in harmony with my success. My success is abnormal. My guilt alerts me to it.

SANDY: (*Into the phone*) Garfield?

HARRY: (*Turns to* SANDY.) So, done is done. What do you say?

SANDY: (*Into the phone*) I got you, shyster! I got you, got you, got you, shyster, shyster, shyster!

(*He hangs up the phone, pops the last bite of sandwich into his mouth, and heads for the door.*)

HARRY: Did you hear what I said?

SANDY: Yeah, you got an island and a mountain.

HARRY: (*Sighs*) Where are you going?

SANDY: Lunch. With the studio. I'm dropping this off and then I'll be back to pick up the Maserati you should buy me. (*At the door*) Harry?

HARRY: What?

SANDY: I love this business.

(*He exits.* HARRY *stands for a moment. He looks at his new typewriter.*)

HARRY: Welcome to my world.

(*We hear a voice calling outside the door.*)

JUSTIN: Thank you! I love you all!

(HARRY *clutches his chest. The door opens and* JUSTIN DEAN *backs into the room. He is ageless, tanned, and wearing a tuxedo and an English accent. He calls out the door.*)

JUSTIN: Thank you! You're wonderful! Really! Thanks! You're marvelous! Thanks!!

HARRY: Who's marvelous?

JUSTIN: My fans.

HARRY: (*Startled*) What?

JUSTIN: Your door was open, we came in. (*He moves to the window.*) Wasn't that Sandy flying out of the house? He got a bit trampled, I'm afraid.

(HARRY *moves to the door and opens it. He stares, wide eyed, and quickly shuts the door on arms and hands holding pens and autograph books.*)

JUSTIN: He screamed at me to stop clogging traffic and get into a limousine where I belong. Isn't that ridiculous! (*Calls out the window.*) I belong to all of you!

HARRY: There are people in my house. (*Worse*) People who admire you.

(JUSTIN *pulls the window curtains closed and looks at* HARRY *across the room, their first actual confrontation. For a moment, a look of absolute despair crosses* JUSTIN'S *face, but he recovers his composure and sits. They regard each other.*)

JUSTIN: I think cordiality is key here.

HARRY: Fine. May I offer you something?

JUSTIN: You may not.

(*They watch each other.*)

JUSTIN: Tell me, Duncan, how is your family?

HARRY: Lori's fine.

JUSTIN: I'm sorry to have missed her.

HARRY: I know she'd love to be here.

JUSTIN: And what news of Beth?

HARRY: Married to someone else.

JUSTIN: Still? Well, unmarried we have in common then, don't we? Of course, I've never been. No family for me, no, never had time for that sort of, expression, as my ties, my dedication, my consummate loyalty lie elsewhere.

(*They both sigh.*)

JUSTIN: If it were mine to do again, progeny, I think.

HARRY: Stop talking like your life is over.

JUSTIN: Hear me out, murderer! I give you twenty-five years and get paid back by stiletto!

HARRY: It has nothing to do with you.

JUSTIN: I turned down *On The Waterfront*, did you know that?

HARRY: Oh please.

JUSTIN: No later than taking my first steps on American soil . . .

ACT ONE

HARRY: Oh please.

JUSTIN: Do I have two scripts thrust into my hands and am immediately faced with a decision that would shape my destiny.

(HARRY *motions to the typewriter that it should listen to this.*)

JUSTIN: Do I do this picture about a young pugilist who runs into a spot of trouble on the Hoboken dockside and becomes hero to his mates, or do I do this spy thing? I was new in town, alone with my luggage and talent, so I put a call in overseas to Olivier because we had made a practice of seeking each other out for career advice. Well, when he got wind who it was ringing him up transatlantic, he dropped everything smack in the middle of the nunnery scene to take the call. Needless to say, this infuriated Jean Simmons, but now we share a chuckle about it over Cinzano. Anyway, I said to him, Larry, I've got this Elia Kazan phoning day and night offering the moon but I've a feeling for this secret agent situation. Well. Do you know what he told me? He told me to follow my instinct because that's what talent does.

HARRY: How fortunate for me.

JUSTIN: So, I called Kazan and turned him down but recommended that Brando chap who did such a nice job on that Polish picture. Fate's funny, n'est ce pas? Marlon goes on to win my Oscar, Larry goes on to be knighted, and I go on to be machine gunned in the back of a taxicab, thank you very much.

HARRY: You actually believe all that, don't you?

JUSTIN: Dear boy, it's common knowledge. They offered me *Waterfront*, they offered me *Casablanca*, they offered me *Ben Hur* . . . When I think what those pictures could have been.

(HARRY *clutches his chest a little.*)

JUSTIN: But you see, there was my devotion to Axel, already taking the colonies by storm. No! I would not confuse my following by captaining a chariot! Now, enough of me half a mo' I've just stopped by to tell you I thoroughly enjoyed *Flirting With Death*. Smashing. Your best effort to date. There are just one or two of the tiniest areas to be rectified if I am to sleep at all tonight.

HARRY: No changes. It's complete. Thank you for coming, it's always a joy.

(*He extends his hand.* JUSTIN *ignores it.*)

JUSTIN: Item one; the garrote in the hatband. Duncan, how many times must I tell you, I do not wear a hat. My tousled hair is our fortune and it is not to be covered up. Are you not considering me at the typewriter?

HARRY: Not for a moment. Not for an instant. When I am at my typewriter I consider my character and it is not within my character to consider you.

JUSTIN: Let's put something right then, shall we? When we speak of Axel Troy, we are speaking of me. I am his visual effect throughout the hemispheres and it has been my life's work to make it so, which brings us to item two; . . . (*He picks up the manuscript.*) What I am to understand, then, on page two hundred fifty seven . . . (*Shows* HARRY *the section.*) . . . here, what you would have me do, is, expire.

HARRY: Yeah.

JUSTIN: I see. Then it's true.

HARRY: Yeah.

JUSTIN: I see. Might we discuss an alternative interpretation?

HARRY: There isn't any.

JUSTIN: I see. Thanks.

HARRY: My pleasure. Have a good trip back.

(*He extends his hand.* JUSTIN *ignores it and stands, squeezing the bridge of his nose.* HARRY *moves to the library, selects a book, and addresses the typewriter.*)

HARRY: Victor Hugo. He wrote in French. You don't have to . . .

(*He reads while* JUSTIN *quivers and snuffles and jerks his head about.*)

HARRY: . . . No one had yet noticed . . . a strange spectator . . . a neck so intently stretched, a face so deformed, that, but for its clothing, half red and half purple, he might have been mistaken for

one of those stone monsters through whose mouths the long gutters of
. . . Notre Dame . . . have disgorged the rains for six hundred years
. . . With the speed of a cat that has leaped from a rooftop, he . . .
picked up the gypsy . . . and with one bound was inside the church,
holding the girl above his head, and crying in a loud voice . . .

JUSTIN: (*Screams*) Megghhgh!

HARRY: (*Looks up*) You all right?

JUSTIN: Yes. Quite all right. Considering I'm having a stroke.

HARRY: No you're not. You're just overacting.

JUSTIN: (*Crazily*) Overacting? Overacting? I've expired with no alternative interpretation! If I'm not going to overact now, when am I going to overact?

(SANDY *blasts through the door, very excited, very happy.*)

SANDY: It's a deal, boys! What's for lunch?

JUSTIN: (*Nose to nose with* SANDY) Megghhgh!

(HARRY *shuts the door on arms and hands and autograph books.*)

SANDY: (*Turns to* HARRY.) What's the matter with him?

HARRY: He's having a stroke.

SANDY: (*Points a stern finger at him.*) You better not.

JUSTIN: (*Gropes for the manuscript.*) You've read this?

SANDY: (*Quickly*) How dare you! (*Turns to* HARRY.) You know you got people in your house?

JUSTIN: (*Squeezing his nose.*) Give me an aspirin. Give me something to relieve this throb.

(HARRY *takes the gun from its stand and points it at* JUSTIN.)

JUSTIN: (*Turns*) Gah! No. Please. I'd rather something less effective.

(HARRY *fires twice. Two aspirin bounce off of* JUSTIN, *onto the floor.* HARRY *replaces the gun.* JUSTIN *picks up the aspirin.*)

JUSTIN: I suppose you found that satisfying.

HARRY: Yeah.

SANDY: Nahh. Let me tell you about satisfying.

(*Two factions.* HARRY *and* JUSTIN *do battle at the desk while* SANDY *is swept away by his own euphoria.*)

HARRY: You want water?

JUSTIN: (*Eats the aspirin.*) I want explanation!

SANDY: Satisfying is being a shark.

JUSTIN: I want a reason why!

SANDY: Satisfying is being a hungry shark, on my left Mr. Publishing Big Shot, on my right Mr. Moving Picture Big Shot.

JUSTIN: Surely you believe you have a good one and I believe I'm entitled to know what it is!

SANDY: Intimidated? Me? Man eater? Which is what a shark is which is what I am—

HARRY: You want to know?

JUSTIN: I want to know!

SANDY: Which is what everybody who is anybody in this town knows!

HARRY: Because it's become too easy! Because there is no question anymore that whatever we turn out is going to succeed. No anxiety. No pacing the floor. No throwing up. Who can live like that?

SANDY: They know, because they first offered me four million little fishies. But the shark says, no! He bides his time.

JUSTIN: That's your reason?

HARRY: Yes.

JUSTIN: And you expect me to understand?

HARRY: No.

SANDY: They know, because they next offered me four and a half million little fishies. But the shark says, no! He circles.

ACT ONE   19

JUSTIN: Because I am well able to live like that and am quite adjusted to fortune smiling upon us.

HARRY: Fortune isn't smiling anymore. it's grinning some hideous grin.

SANDY: They know, because they placed before me five million fishies . . . and I ate 'em alive and swam away . . . satisfied.

HARRY: What we are now is what we will be forever unless we recognize the time to move on. Don't you recognize the time to move on?

JUSTIN: (*Horrified*) No!!

SANDY: (*Ecstatic*) OH!! The shark, babe, has such teeth dear, and he shows them, pearly white!

(*He sings, dances, and snaps his fingers as he offers a stunning rendition of* "Mack The Knife". *He is lost in his joy and oblivious to the conversation taking place on the other side of the room.*)

JUSTIN: What we are now is what I want to be forever! The object of fascination to my crowd outside!

HARRY: This has nothing to do with your crowd outside!

JUSTIN: It bloody well has everything to do with them! Their acceptance is our success. They accept you. What more is there?

HARRY: My acceptance. I want to accept me!

JUSTIN: Too late. You've given them a hero. He's theirs now and you haven't the right to snatch him away in some effort to punish the public for some private demons driving you.

HARRY: Demons?

JUSTIN: Of course. Demons. Spirits. Everybody has spirits. I have spirits, he has spirits.

SANDY: Oooooooh Miss Lotte Len . . . YA! And that 'ol Lucy Brown . . .

JUSTIN: He has lots of spirits. (*Wheels on* SANDY.) You lunatic. Do you know what you've done?

SANDY: (*In tempo*) What I done! Hey! The shark bites. Whoa! Pretty teeth, dear . . . (*Bares his teeth.*) Yah, yah, yah, yah, yah, yah, rah, dah, bum . . .

JUSTIN: (*Shoves the manuscript at* SANDY.) You're telling me you've read this?

SANDY: (*Takes the manuscript. Kisses it. Big finish.*) Now that Mackie's . . . back in towwwn!

JUSTIN: (*Withdrawn. Fetal.*) I can't believe it. You work, you give, you sweat, you bleed . . .

SANDY: What's to believe? (*Tosses the manuscript onto the desk.*) What's to read?

(JUSTIN *freezes.*)

SANDY: (*Picks up the phone.*) I'm not going back in today. (*Dials*) In fact, I just might take the rest of my life off.

JUSTIN: What's to read?

SANDY: (*Into the phone*) Yeah, Doll, it's me. Who called?

JUSTIN: What's to read?

SANDY: (*Into the phone*) MGM? Universal? I'll buy 'em.

JUSTIN: (*Nose to nose with* SANDY) Whatstoread?

SANDY: (*Into the phone*) Hold on, Doll. (*To* JUSTIN) You know, you've really got to do something about that.

JUSTIN: HA! (*Looks at* SANDY.) HA HA! (*Hysterically*) HAAAH! (*His eyes fill with tears as he laughs and cries, calms down, and looks at* SANDY, *spent.*) You idiot.

SANDY: (*To* HARRY) What's he doing here, anyway? (*To* JUSTIN) You're upset, am I right?

JUSTIN: HA HA HA HA!

SANDY: (*Trying to catch on*) What'd you do, Harry? Dream up another trick hat? (*Chuckles*) You and your trick hats, I tell you. Will you stop with the trick hats. Look what it does to him.

JUSTIN: (*Seething*) Read it!? You haven't even looked at it!

SANDY: All right, I skipped a couple areas. I got it sold. You're in business. What do you want from me?

JUSTIN: (*Turns on* HARRY.) And you knew he wouldn't read it! How could you not tell him?

HARRY: I told him.

JUSTIN: How?

HARRY: I told him to his face.

JUSTIN: (*Horrified*) To his face?? They don't understand anything to their face! You have to tell them over the phone!

SANDY: (*Suspiciously*) Something's the matter.

JUSTIN: Why don't you ask your assistant what she thought of *Flirting With Death*.

SANDY: (*Into phone*) So Doll. Harry's new one. Winner, huh? (*To* HARRY *and* JUSTIN) Yeah, she says, winner. And she's very sorry. (*Back into phone*) What are you sorry about, Doll?

(SANDY *stands, smiling broadly. He is clutching the receiver to his ear as his smile turns into a hideous gargoyle grin and he freezes, stone still. He does not move, except his eyes. In his eyes is panic.*)

HARRY: (*Crosses to him.*) Sandy. You have to understand. Who will if you won't? (*Comforts him*) Remember when we started together? Nobody wanted to handle me because all I dreamed of being was a great novelist and they said, forget great, great doesn't sell until after you're dead and who wants to wait that long? But you said that I could be great but first write a commercial book and I didn't have to use my real name! Just one commercial book and don't worry because you didn't know if you could sell it anyway. And I said, what if you do sell it? And you said, so it'll bring in enough money to pay the rent. Sandy, I didn't know you meant forever!

JUSTIN: (*Sitting despondently on the sofa.*) I could've been a contender.

HARRY: Now it's sixteen books later, . . . (*Studies* SANDY's *gargoyle face.*) . . . and here is fourtune's smile. (*To* SANDY) You are a big literary agent. (*To* JUSTIN) And you're a movie star. And nobody knows me by my real name. (*To* SANDY) You got what you wanted—

JUSTIN: All I got is a one-way ticket to Palookaville.

HARRY: And with all I've got, I don't know how I got it at all!

JUSTIN: You're hardly in position to merit sympathy.

HARRY: I don't want to merit sympathy. I want to know what I did to merit the position. (*To* SANDY) And I want you to understand what I'm doing. Okay?

SANDY: (*Frozen. Grinning.*) Okay. (HARRY *takes the receiver from* SANDY's *hand.*)

HARRY: (*Into the phone*) He'll have to call you back, Doll.

JUSTIN: (*Taunting*) They gave you five million?

SANDY: (*Frozen. Grinning.*) Harry.

JUSTIN: They'd given you twenty five million!

SANDY: (*Frozen. Grinning.*) Harry.

JUSTIN: They'd've given you the keys to the studio!

SANDY: (*Frozen. Grinning.*) I forget how to breathe.

HARRY: You can't forget how to breathe.

SANDY: (*Frozen. Grinning.*) Goodbye, Harry,

HARRY: I knew you'd take it like this.

SANDY: (*Frozen. Grinning.*) Goodbye, Harry.

HARRY: If I didn't need you to understand, would you remember how to breathe?

SANDY: (*Frozen. Grinning.*) Very fast. (HARRY *sighs.*)

SANDY: (*Frozen. Grinning.*) I don't have to understand anymore?

HARRY: No. You did good.

(SANDY's *face muscles relax. He takes deep breaths and loosens up. He smiles warmly at* HARRY. *He chuckles. Stops.*)

SANDY: May I see that, please?

(*He takes the manuscript, turns to the last page, and reads.*)

SANDY: Rah de rah de rah, taxicab, KGB, machine guns, rah de rah . . . he figures he was dead. No broad was that good. The end. (*Looks for more.*) Where's the rest of it?

HARRY: There isn't any.

SANDY: (*Looks at the manuscript.*) The end? He's dead the end?

HARRY: The end.

SANDY: (*To* JUSTIN) He's dead the end. That the part that bothers you?

JUSTIN: Right.

SANDY: Right. Bothers me, too.

(*He rips it out of the manuscript, crumples it up, and gets rid of it. He turns to* HARRY.)

Kiddo. Listen. Got to be honest with you. He's dead the end? Stinks. Take my word for it. Whooee boy. Stinko. I don't even have to read the rest of it because I know it's great. Attaboy Harry, great stuff. You just take an hour and fix that last part up. (*Turns*) Justin, let's go, buddy. Harry's fixing it up. All right? Fine.

(*He turns to go. He stops. He stands still. He screams. He wheels on* HARRY.)

SANDY: What!?

HARRY: I'm through.

SANDY: You're through? How can you be through? I'm not through. You're only the client!

JUSTIN: No, no. You're going at this like a businessman. This must be approached on the level of the artist. Duncan, as one to another, you can't be through because writing is not a profession from which one may simply retire. You're in it for life. Axel doesn't die. You die. You collapse over your typewriter at too young an age in the middle of your new book. Everyone knows that. It's expected of you.

SANDY: Really well put. (*To* HARRY) You know, it's not too late to bring in Paul Newman, would that change your mind?

HARRY: He's right. If Ernest Hemingway was a mailman I wonder if he would've put a gun in his mouth. I never used to understand what got in the way of his clarity. Or why Edgar Allen Poe went nuts. I realize these are exceptions, it's just that they happen to be among my favorite writers, along with Virginia Woolf who walked into the ocean. I refuse to read Sylvia Plath because I'm terrified I might admire her work. All of a sudden I'm fifty-one years old. Fifty was good. We had a party. Now I'm fifty-one. It's relentless. Sandy. I'm frightened by these recent flashes of understanding the suicidal point of view. It's time to kill somebody. It's him or me.

SANDY: He's not right! You never wanted to be like any of those people. Those people are crazy. You wanted to be like Mark Twain. Dickens! How did he die?

(HARRY *picks up the book on his desk and tosses it to* SANDY *who opens it, finds a place, and reads.*)

SANDY: . . . Rah de rah, born, improvidence, hunger, deprivation, rah de rah . . . His last novel, *Edwin Drood* was left unfinished as he collapsed and died after a full day's work. He was fifty-eight years old. (*Closes the book.*) All right, forget him.

HARRY: All I wanted to do was write a good book and now there's a ghost in the house.

JUSTIN: But, why must you do away with him? Why can't you just put him aside awhile?

HARRY: I've tried. I can't. He's everywhere I go. My day begins with little Alex Troy dolls as free gifts in my breakfast cereal.

SANDY: (*Brightly*) Three hundred grand they paid us!

HARRY: I see the children walking to school carry Axel Troy lunchboxes.

SANDY: Half a million against ten percent!

HARRY: I go to the movies, there's an Axel Troy film festival. I turn on the television, he's in reruns (*Softly*) I've never mentioned this to anyone but late one night, some months back, I looked out my window and saw him. Lots of him. Midgets. Axel midgets running down the street heading for my house. The doorbell rang. I jumped behind my desk and didn't come out. The doorbell kept ringing and ringing!

(HARRY *stares out the window.* JUSTIN *looks to* SANDY.)

SANDY: The Axel Troy Halloween costume! A gold mine.

JUSTIN: And you're just going to let it all disappear?

SANDY: I'm torn, Justin. I'm really torn. Look at him. (*He holds out his hand as if it were a scale.*) On one hand there's friendship, loyalty, trust in our working relationship, on the other hand . . . (*He holds the other hand higher, lighter, outweighed.*) . . . what are we talking about? Money?

JUSTIN: Lots of money.

SANDY: (*Brings his hands to an even position.*) All right, lots of money. Still, my advice has to be carefully measured. I'm dealing with the fragile sensitivities of talent. I want to be certain of my values before I make a move. (*He considers one hand.*) Friendship. Loyalty. Trust. (*He considers the other hand.* JUSTIN *hangs over his shoulder.*)

JUSTIN: Lots of money.

SANDY: Friendship.

JUSTIN: Lots of money

SANDY: Loyalty.

JUSTIN: Lots of money

SANDY: Trust.

JUSTIN: Lots of money

(SANDY *struggles as the money hand has grown progressively heavier, and finally topples the scale.*)

SANDY: Money it is. (*Looks at* JUSTIN, *seriously.*) I tried. I tried very hard.

JUSTIN: You were terrific.

(SANDY *flicks away the items in the outweighed hand, picks up the phone, and dials.*)

SANDY: Gloria, give me Garfield. (*Sweetly*) Gar? Hi fella, how's the boy? (*To* JUSTIN) He's laughing. He knows. (*Back into the phone*) Fella? I bet you heard a little rumor from the studio today. (*Aghast*) You heard it at the Tea Room? (*To* JUSTIN) It's all over town already! (*Into the phone*) Well good, good. I decided to let this one go charitably because I'm a pussycat and I want everybody to know it. (*To* JUSTIN) He's laughing very hard. (*Into the phone*) They were ready to buy it for how much??

(*He grabs the gun from its stand and spills fifty aspirin onto the desk. He scoops them up and is about to swallow them all but* JUSTIN *grabs his wrist. Even so,* SANDY *manages to raise them close to his open mouth.* JUSTIN *uses two hands to make him drop them on the desk.*)

SANDY: (*Into the phone*) Hey, I got five up front, right? I'll see the rest of it eventually. What do you mean, not in this lifetime? (*To* JUSTIN) He's trying to irritate me. You let me know if I lose control because that's what he wants. (*Sweetly into the phone*) Gar? Know what? Fine. Why shouldn't I sound remarkably calm? I feel good. Why do I feel good? (*Explodes*) Because you're going to get me out of this deal, that's why!

(JUSTIN *taps him on the shoulder.*)

SANDY: Harry'll pay you your lousy forty thousand and he'll never pull anything cute on you again.

(JUSTIN *has his attention.* SANDY *motions he's okay.*)

SANDY: I'll ruin him. (*Calmly back into the phone.*) All right, fifty thousand. All right, sixty. Seventy! What do you mean you can't get us out??

(JUSTIN *taps him on the shoulder.*)

SANDY: I am talking eighty Swiss bank thousand dollars you scum!

(JUSTIN *has his attention.* SANDY *motions he's okay.*)

SANDY: Why doesn't it matter how much I'm talking? Yeah the contracts are signed and delivered, I delivered them myself. (*Yells*) Just what is so funny?

(JUSTIN *taps him on the shoulder.* SANDY *grabs his finger and drives him to his knees.*)

SANDY: All right! You want funny?? Here's funny! You don't get me out of this deal, I throw Ma right out of my house. She has no other children Garfield, whose doorstep you figure she'll end up on? How come you're not laughing anymore? (*Laughs*) No, no, you don't get any money now. All you get is Ma. She comes equipped with three canasta ladies, three Mah Jongg ladies, and a wet hacking cough that splits the night like a siren! So talk to me! (*Smiles at* JUSTIN.) There is a way? I knew you could do it, little Brother. Under what? Duress? If he was harassed into signing, it's no good? (*Jubilant*) That's it! We're clear. He was definitely harassed! Absolutely I can prove it, I was the one who harassed him. (*To* JUSTIN) He's hysterical. (*Into the phone*) Go ahead! Enjoy yourself! Because tonight I'm dropping off a package. I'm dropping off a package, Garfield, you hear me? Listen to this! (*He slams the phone down three times, looks at it, and picks it up.*) Hello? (*He holds up the receiver.*) This phone is broken.

(SANDY *and* JUSTIN *look at each other. They sit, disconsolate.* HARRY *turns from the window.*)

HARRY: Thomas Wolfe died from tuberculosis of the brain. This was the same brain that had given us *Look Homeward, Angel* and *You Can't Go Home Again* all before he was thirty seven because that's when he left us. And he didn't want to go, either. So, whether you understand or don't, after you've given it some thought I'm sure you'll come around.

SANDY: (*Jumps up and embraces him.*) What thought? I'm around already! Who need thought among friends?

JUSTIN: (*Jumps up*) What??

SANDY: (*To* JUSTIN) You, are a dead man. He, is still alive. (*His hands again become scales.*) Alive. Dead. (*Alive outweighs dead*) Harry, what you want, I want.

JUSTIN: Oh. Well. This is fine. This is splendid.

SANDY: Face it. You're finished. Lie down.

JUSTIN: Finished? Finished, you say?

(*This triggers something in* JUSTIN. *He relaxes. He chuckles and looks at* HARRY *and at* SANDY. *He seems, all of a sudden, to have taken on new stature. He has become his on-screen interpretation of Axel Troy.*)

JUSTIN: Gentlemen. You are no doubt aware that I have been thought finished before. I have faced representative assassins from each continent on Earth, yet I remain. I have found myself placed in every imaginable life-and-death situation, yet I am unmarked. Do you really expect me to believe the coup de grace is to come from some aging pulp novelist and his parasite? Gentlemen, I sneer. (*He sneers.*) I chuckle.

(*He chuckles. He spins and reaches into his boot and come up with his finger. His movement is fluid, perfect. He fires twice.*)

JUSTIN: (*At* HARRY) BANG! (*At* SANDY) BANG! (*He exits.*)

HARRY: Aging pulp novelist.

SANDY: Yeah, but you're the best there is.

HARRY: Parasite.

SANDY: Yeah, but I'm the best there is.

HARRY: That's what I sell. Pulp. I don't sell hardcover do I, Sandy?

SANDY: I always get you a nice hardcover deal.

HARRY: A gift to secure paperback rights. You know that. How much am I worth, hardcover alone?

(SANDY *groans.*)

HARRY: I've sold a billion paperbacks and sixteen hardcovers. (*Points to them on the desk.*) And there they are. I want to come up with something I'd be proud to put in my library.

SANDY: (*Sighs*) So, when do you figure this masterwork to be completed?

HARRY: Who can tell? A month A year.

SANDY: (*Panicky*) A year? I can't stop negotiating for a year! You've got to give me a period of withdrawal!

HARRY: But I have nothing for you now.

SANDY: Let me sell your car!

HARRY: Sandy?

ACT ONE

SANDY: What?

HARRY: Do you have demons?

SANDY: What?

HARRY: Spirits. Inside you. Making you do things you might not really want to do.

SANDY: No.

HARRY: Why not?

SANDY: Because there are two kinds of people in the world: people who have demons and people who are demons. And I'm yours. I'm your demon.

HARRY: (*Smiles*) No, whoever my demons are, they have a bigger piece of me than ten percent. (*Shows him to the door.*) Anyway, this gives you time to haunt your other clients.

SANDY: Who?

HARRY: You have other clients.

SANDY: Yeah? Maybe one of them wants to go to lunch. (*He starts off, and turns to look at his friend.*)

SANDY: Harry.

HARRY: Yeah?

SANDY: Don't go crazy.

(*He exits.* HARRY *shuts the door and moves to his library. He stands, facing his store of books, looking them over. He turns and sits at his desk. He takes a piece of paper and puts it into his typewriter. He types. Stops. Looks at paper.*)

HARRY: (*Reads*) 1945. My life, like the lake, was frozen over. I looked to the sky. The moon fell down and no one could find it. (*He looks at typewriter.*) What are you talking about? (*He reloads it and types. Stops. Reads.*) Time was short, and so was Benny.

(*Fade out*)

End of Act One

ACT TWO

Scene One

(*Late that evening*)

(HARRY *as we left him, except he is dressed in sweater and slacks. He holds a drink in his hands. There is a bottle of whiskey in front of him, well on its way to empty. He is drowning in a sea of crumpled typing paper. It lies all over the room, like dust. He surveys the crumpled paper and speaks to the typewriter.*)

HARRY: A tree. A whole tree you've lain to waste. (*He looks at the typewriter pitifully.*) I think this masterpiece business is new to you is what, so I'm going to tell you all you need to know to feel part of it and we can get started. (*Rises and refills his glass.*) These are the generations of the written word. In the beginning there was Greece. Greece begat Aeschylus who wrote tragedy, Aristophones who wrote comedy, and Aristotle who told us which was which. Tragedia and comedia have been the basis for writing, since. Now, Greece gave way to Rome, which gave us Ovid who wrote of love. Love, then, would fall into one of the two aforementioned categories but with Aristotle dead, mankind has been left forever guessing which one. Rome fell and we found ourselves in the Dark Ages, a time of guiltless barbarism and wild sexual abandon. From this era of moral degradation sprung Dante's *Inferno*, a tale of souls roasting in torment as payment rendered for squandering precious life. This sobered everybody up pretty good for the Renaissance. Thomas More, John Donne, Leonardo Da Vinci . . . Pinpointing the end of this glorious era has been left in some dispute but it is believed to have been brought to a close after William Shakespeare and before myself. Now you know everything. Let's see what you can do.

(*He puts a piece of paper into the typewriter and stares at it a moment. He types, slowly at first and gradually reaching blazing speed until we realize he is randomly pushing buttons. He pulls the paper out of the typewriter and examines it.*)

Act Two

HARRY: Nothing. (*He crumples it up and tosses it into the air. He puts his feet on the desk and holds the drink in his hands, as he was. The door opens. LORI enters, dressed up and beautiful.*)

LORI: I saw the light on and thought I'd check up on you.

HARRY: Thanks. How'm I doing?

LORI: (*Looks around the room.*) Not so good, huh?

(*She uncrumples a piece of paper at her feet and reads.*) Call me Ishmael . . . Dad, this is *Moby Dick*.

HARRY: (*Dumbfounded. To the typewriter.*) And I yelled at you? Forgive, me, buddy.

LORI: I don't think drinking is going to do it.

HARRY: Has to. It's the natural second step. Step one, I suffer. I sleep on the floor. Step two, I drink.

LORI: Step three?

HARRY: I pick up my Pulitzer Prize. I've done research. I have found that a startling common denominator in the biographies of our great writers is the drunken evening, folded over a wood table, a stub pencil, and cheap whiskey.

LORI: (*Picks up the bottle.*) This is Chivas Regal.

HARRY: It'll have to do.

LORI: You go to bed.

HARRY: No. I want to write about sled dogs.

LORI: You've locked yourself in this room and you haven't slept and now you're drinking and you don't drink.

HARRY: I know. I have serious catching up to do. Ask Dylan Thomas. Ask Lewis Carroll.

LORI: I didn't know Lewis Carroll drank.

HARRY: (*Confidentially*) Neither did I until I read this . . . (*He picks up a book, opened to a particular passage. He reads.*) 'Twas brilling and the slithy toves did gyre and gimble in the wabe.

LORI: That's Jabberwocky.

HARRY: I'll say it is. Now, I have been awakened in the middle of the night by an idea and sleepily written down my thought, only to rise in the morning and on the paper find slithy toves all brilling in the gimble. But, I never had the presence of mind not to throw it away. Well, one man's garbage is another man's wonderland. Let's talk about you, Alice.

LORI: Stephen took me to a fancy restaurant.

HARRY: That's dinner. He took you to fancy dinner and you let him. How long have you been seeing this boy?

LORI: Ten months.

HARRY: This is just the sort of thing that leads to dancing. Dinner, dancing and then—

LORI: The back of the ol' taxicab.

HARRY: You said it.

LORI: I stand warned.

HARRY: I think it's time we talked, you and I.

LORI: (*Sits by him. Takes his hand.*) You're in no condition to think.

HARRY: I'm fine. Sit down. This is the kind of talk a father usually has with his son, which I don't have because your mother took off without the common decency of giving me one, as you know. Not that I wanted a son more than I wanted you of course, I've just always wanted to have this talk. (*Looks at her.*) You remember your mother?

LORI: Dad, I speak to her three times a week.

HARRY: In Utah?

LORI: Uh huh.

HARRY: She skis, there. She's a skier. I bought her a mountain, what did she want from me? In the middle of the night when her husband gets ideas, he turn to her instead of a typewriter. That's what she wanted from me. (*Turns to her*) Why do you stay here when you could be a skier in Utah?

LORI: I don't ski.

ACT TWO

HARRY: What do you do?

LORI: I help you.

HARRY: Why?

LORI: Because you're helpless.

HARRY: I'm not helpless. I just let you think I'm helpless so you'll make me breakfast.

LORI: I enjoy it.

HARRY: You're too old to enjoy it. I understood it when you were a little girl and made me cereal and I understood it when your mother decided to hit the slopes and you made me waffles for a year. I was very consoled by those waffles. How come you like me so much? How come you're not begging me to let you live in some one-room place downtown with bars on the windows and rusty water?

LORI: I like the water here.

HARRY: But I'm depriving you of the chance to find a job and fulfill your potential and become the total woman.

LORI: I have a job.

HARRY: Helping me is no job.

LORI: Says you.

HARRY: Then you should have a title.

LORI: Executive Daughter.

HARRY: Then you should have a salary.

LORI: Whatever you think I'm worth.

HARRY: I don't have that kind of money.

LORI: I'll wait you out. I've heard you're talented.

HARRY: (*Reflects*) She was hesitant to marry me because she was afraid I might be talented. Lori. Take it from your mother. Marry someone with absolutely no talent. Marry Justin. (*He puts a new sheet of paper into the typewriter and stares at it.*)

LORI: Dad?

HARRY: I'm fine. I'm ready to work. I've depressed myself to the point of writing great comedy.

(*He stares at the typewriter. She moves to the door, watching him. He stares at the typewriter. She exits, quietly closing the door. He passes out. Lights change. Softer shades.*)

(*A boy and girl, both about fourteen years old, appear within the room. He wears a student's jacket, shirt, striped and patched pants, all wrinkled but of good quality. He is barefoot. She wears a party dress and her hair is ribboned. Her shoes are polished and he fingernails are clean. He explores the room. She stays where she is, more reserved.*)

TOM: (*Taken with the room*) Some fancy marbles, huh?

BECKY: (*Peeking around*) I bet the rugging tickles your feet.

TOM: Feels good all right, 'tween th' toes. Whyn't y' take your own shoes off?

BECKY: Because a proper young lady don't go 'round barefoot in other people's fine houses is why I don't.

TOM: Well, hang it. I thank my stars I weren't made no proper young lady. Elsewise I s'pose I shouldn't jump up on this elegant sofa, here. (*He leaps onto the couch.*)

BECKY: Oh now, don't.

TOM: (*Standing on his head.*) Well?

BECKY: You don't impress me and you never will, neither.

TOM: Y'know, after a hundred years tryin' I'm a mind t' believe you.

(*He flips onto the floor.* HARRY *looks up, bright and alert.*)

BECKY: See? Now y' gone and woke him.

HARRY: Hey!

TOM: Hey yourself mister and give me an apple.

BECKY: (*To* TOM) You just wait 'til you are offered and don't be so impolite. (*To* HARRY) We 'pologize.

HARRY: How'd you two get in here?

ACT TWO

TOM: Two?

(*He looks around the room and at* BECKY.)

BECKY: (*Moves in on* HARRY *and peers at him.*) Oh yes, he's right here, 'tween his eyeballs, wavin' to me.

(TOM *pours a drink, finishing the bottle.*)

HARRY: All right, now just wait—

TOM: (*Force feeds him.*) All right, now you wait just and drink down this here corn and do's your told!

(*Another boy pops up in another part of the room. He is a little more vagrant. Straw hat, suspenders, ripped jeans which hang in shards draping his shins. There is a corn cob pipe in his back pocket. He carries a dead cat by its tail. He is agitated.*)

HUCK: 'Bout time, pards. I was wond'rin' if you's gone run off'n yer own selfs an' left me inside altogether.

(HUCK *sniffs, looks around, and notices the bottle of whiskey on the desk. He hands the cat to* HARRY, *takes the bottle, and turns it to his mouth.*)

HUCK: None left. (*Looks at* HARRY) Don't y' think that's jes' a might obnoxious?

(HARRY *regards the children.*)

HARRY: I know who you are.

HARRY: (*To* TOM) Didn't take him such a long time t' figger us out, did it?

TOM: (*Reminds him*)! We well knowed.

HUCK: Oh yeah.

HARRY: (*Looking over the cat.*) What's this?

HUCK: My cat. What'll y' gimme for it?

HARRY: It's dead.

HUCK: Costs extra.

(*He puts the cat down on the desk.* BECKY *is at the library, looking through the books.*)

TOM: Can't y' find 'em?

BECKY: Just give me a spell.

HARRY: What are you looking for?

HUCK: She's lookin' for th' 'ventures of hisself and myself.

HARRY: Of course. I have them both.

(*He steps on the ladder and lifts* BECKY *to a higher shelf.*)

HARRY: You look just like I've always imagined.

BECKY: (*Takes down two leatherbound books.*) Obliged.

(TOM *is intrigued by the ladder. He climbs on it and rides across the room.*)

HARRY: (*To* BECKY) You're welcome. (*Proudly*) They're signed editions.

HUCK: (*Startled*) What?

HARRY: Yes, very valuable, because if you open the, let me show you, you see, he's signed them, here.

HUCK: Who did?

HARRY: Mark Twain.

HUCK: He wrote on my book?

HARRY: (*Shows him*) Right here.

HUCK: He wrote on my clean book?

HARRY: But that's what makes it so valuable.

HUCK: I'm what makes it so valuable. What's a matter with you?

TOM: (*Gliding over the ladder.*) Now, settle down. He dasn't know what he's sayin'.

HUCK: (*Taking the book from* HARRY.) Lemme have a look on this here.

HARRY: And what makes it especially rare is what he's written. Can you read that?

HUCK: A course I c'n read that. (*Hands it to* TOM.) What's it say, there?

ACT TWO 37

TOM: Says, afe'tionately, Samuel.

HUCK: So?

HARRY: So? (*Takes the book. Shows them.*) So, Samuel!

(*The children stare at him.*)

HARRY: Clemens!

HUCK: What good's a Clemens if it's a Twain on the cover?

HARRY: Because everybody knows Mark Twain's real name is Samuel Clemens!

(*The children stare at each other and mumble amongst themselves.*)

TOM: That a fact?

BECKY: Never mentioned it to me.

HUCK: Alla time y' think y' know somebody.

HARRY: You're kidding.

HUCK: Y' mean t' say all them books that jes' say Twain aint's good's this'n here?

HARRY: No, it's not that they're not as good, they're all the same book.

HUCK: Well a course they are. And they'll allus be th' same book f'rever and nobody's gonna change a word, 'cept if they's a mind t' scibble up th' inside like this here Clemens.

BECKY: (*Shyly*) May I have that back, please?

(HARRY *surrnders the book to her.*)

HUCK: I s'pose we 'bout ready t' head off, then.

TOM: We got what we come for.

HARRY: My books? You came for my books? Why?

BECKY: (*To* HARRY, *as* LORI *before.*) Why couldn't he just have been shot once neatly through the heart?

HARRY: (*To* BECKY, *startled.*) You know about Axel?

Tom: Pers'nal friends.

Huck: We go fishin'.

Harry: Axel doesn't fish.

Huck: Not anymore. He ups and dies in th' last book.

Becky: And not very nicely, neither.

Tom: We s'posed t' go on forever, y'know.

Huck: Th' last. Ain't it?

Harry: Of course it's the last. He's dead.

Tom: What's that got t' do with it?

Becky: He could live in the next book.

Harry: People wouldn't believe it.

Huck: People'll believe anything they's a mind t' s'long's it suits 'em. And Axel Troy suits 'em fine elsewhere y' wouldn't be wearnin' such fancies. See, when folks think on us here, they's content we havin' some fine time up one river bank or 'nother. But now, when they think on Axel, they's bound t' think on him gone. Not th' livin' but th' diein'. Because it was his last gran' gesture. All on 'count'a one book, which ain't such a good'un neither since they all been goin' downhill lately if y' want th' truth of it.

Harry: (*Struck*) Who says??

Becky: You says. You says inside, where we been.

Huck: Y' knows it 'tween your eyes where I jes' come from. Lately y' jes' been scribblin'.

Tom: Like this Clemens y' made up!

Becky: Now, if y'll 'scuse us, we 'spected somewhere else.

Harry: Where do you go?

Becky: (*Holds up the books.*) We give these here to some little boy learnin' us right now by a light under the blankets.

Harry: That's how I did.

Act Two

HUCK: Of course. And y' held on t' us tight. Tighter'n most care to.

HARRY: (*To* HUCK) We spent time on the raft. (*To* TOM) In the caves. (*To* BECKY. *A confidence.*) I've loved you since I was a boy.

(TOM *looks at* HUCK. BECKY *turns to* HUCK.)

HUCK: Mmn. Most times it's easier settin' off. Growin' up so clouds the' insides, nobody much notices out floatin' away. (*At the library, looking over the books.*) But you, your insides got so filled with us, there weren't no room for much else t' break its way in.

TOM: But now, with Axel gone and you thinkin' thoughts about masterpieces, well, you gonna need all th' room y' c'n get.

HUCK: We jes' come collectin' what's rightly ours and we'll leave y' alone.

HARRY: I don't want you to leave me alone.

HUCK: That ain't th' way we see it.

BECKY: Us, nor Christopher Robin nor Lemuel Gulliver nor Peter Pan nor Tiny Tim.

HUCK: They'll all be by t' pick up their own, directly.

HARRY: Tiny Tim is mad at me?

BECKY: Heartbroken. He set by hisself. He says, God bless Us, Every One.

TOM: Like in th' story.

HARRY: I know where it's from.

TOM: Not anymore y' don't.

HARRY: Huh?

HUCK: I wouldn't bother tryin' t' remember th' stories no more. Because y' won't recall.

HARRY: Why? Because you're stealing my books? Well, you can't. All you are is whiskey in my empty stomach and I don't want to talk to you anymore.

TOM: It's not the books we come for.

HARRY: I want to talk to Mr. Dickens. Bring him out here.

TOM: You don't have him in you.

(HARRY *glares at him and turns away. He notices the area of the library where the books were removed.*)

HARRY: Wait. (*He pulls down two leatherbound books.*) They're still here. You didn't even get the right—

(*He stops and looks at* BECKY *who also holds two leatherbound books. Troubled.*)

HARRY: What do you mean, it's not the books you came for?

HUCK: Y' jes' shakin' up th' river! Y' jes' complicatin' what's natural! I won't never understand you growed ups.

TOM: We come for your recollections.

(HARRY *looks at them, coming to grips with their purpose in his room.*)

HUCK: Scatter!

HARRY: No!

(HARRY *moves toward* BECKY *and reaches for the books. She tosses one to* TOM *and the other to* HUCK. *The boys run off.* HARRY *catches* BECKY *and wraps his arms around her, holding her tightly to him.* BECKY *lifts one of his arms and bites him,* HARRY *yowls, and lets her go. She runs after* TOM *and* HUCK. HARRY *tries to follow but makes it only as far as his desk. He collapses into his chair and passes out, as before. The door opens.*)

(LORI *enters and turns on a light. She is dressed in bed clothes.*)

LORI: Dad?

HARRY: (*Mumbles*) I don't want you to leave me alone!

LORI: (*Move to him.*) I won't. I wouldn't.

(*She lifts his head and cradles it in her hands.* HARRY *is now completely drunk and senseless.*)

HARRY: (*Looks into her eyes.*) I've loved you since I was a little boy!

LORI: Oh gosh. No, Dad, it's Lori.

HARRY: It's Lori?

ACT TWO

LORI: Yes.

HARRY: (*Heartfelt*) I love you too, Lori.

LORI: I know.

HARRY: But not since I was a boy.

LORI: I understand.

(*She rolls the chair,* HARRY *in it, toward the couch.*)

HARRY: Becky Thatcher hates me now.

LORI: (*Dumps him out of the chair, onto the couch.*) She does? And what makes you think that?

HARRY: She was here. She told me.

LORI: (*Comforting him*) She's not here anymore.

HARRY: None of them are here anymore. Because of Axel.

LORI: Well where do you suppose they went?

HARRY: Utah. Skiing. With your mother. She got everything!

LORI: Mmn. We'll talk about it tomorrow over coffee and aspirin. (*She rises.*) I'm looking forward to a fascinating story.

HARRY: (*Suddenly frightened*) I don't know the story! (*He gets off of the couch and makes his way to his typewriter.*) I don't know the stories anymore! (*To the typewriter*) The Adventures of Huckleberry Finn. Author unknown. Chapter One. You don't know about me . . . (*Sadly*) They've come to take their books away! (*He climbs all the way up the library ladder.*) Sanc-tu-ar-y!

(LORI *looks at him, wide eyed, her hands covering her mouth.*)

HARRY: I don't feel good.

(*His head droops.* LORI *Pulls the ladder across the room.* HARRY *steps off of it and lies on the couch.* LORI *turns down the light and sits on the edge of the couch and watches him as he drifts back to sleep. The room is quiet except the clock ticking.* HUCKLEBERRY FINN *shoots up, just behind the couch.*)

HARRY: (*In his sleep*) Ahhh!

HUCK: Forgot my cat.

(HUCK *moves to the desk and picks up the cat. He ties it to a belt loop by its tail.* HARRY *mumbles in discomfort.* LORI *tries to soothe him.*)

LORI: No. Shh. It's just your imagination.

(HUCK *pulls his corn cob pipe from his pocket and packs it as he crosses back behind the couch. He regards* HARRY.)

HUCK: She's right, Harry. It's just your imagination. (*He strikes a match and puffs on the pipe. The soft glow from the flame illuminate the area.*) And it's just leaving!

(HARRY *sits upright. He stares out, frightened.* HUCK *blows out the match. The room is dark.*)

(*The curtain falls.*)

Scene Two

(HARRY's *study — three months later — a midsummer afternoon.*)

(*The books sit neatly on the library shelves. There is no crumpled typewriter paper to be seen.* HARRY *stands by an open window, looking outside.*)

MOVIE DIRECTOR: (*O.S.*) Ready, and . . . Action!

(*Sounds of screeching tires, slamming car doors, machine gun fire, broken glass, more slamming doors and cars screeching off.*)

MOVIE DIRECTOR: (*O.S.*) Cut! That's a wrap. Thank you, all.

(HARRY *shuts the window and turns from it, attempting a forced satisfaction, but his knees buckle and he sits down, staring out blankly. The door to the room bursts open and* JUSTIN *enters, seething. He marches to* HARRY *and spreads his arms to show the front of his tuxedo, peppered with bullet holes. He spins around to reveal the stilettos in his back, and spins again to face* HARRY *and emit some indescribable sound from the depths of his outrage. He exits in a huff.* HARRY *sits, and the room is quiet, except the clock ticking.* LORI *enters, holding a new manuscript.*)

LORI: The book was released today.

HARRY: (*Bemused*) You mean the world is now aware of Axel's demise and yet it goes on spinning?

LORI: Barely. (*She turns on the radio.*)

RADIO STUDIO ANNOUNCER: (*V.O.*) W.A.G.L. News At Noon: He figured he was dead. No broad was that good . . . With these haunting words, Axel Troy, guardian of the free world, is gone. The nation will sleep a little less soundly, tonight.

HARRY: Oh, come on.

RADIO STUDIO ANNOUNCER: (*V.O.*) For public reaction, we switch to our man in the street.

STREET ANNOUNCER: (*V.O.*) (*Exterior; City noises*) Sir! You Sir, have you heard the news about Axel Troy?

MAN: (*V.O.*) Hasn't everybody? What a thing!

(*The voice is familiar.* HARRY *and* LORI *perk up.*)

RADIO STREET ANNOUNCER: (*V.O.*) And would you care to comment?

MAN: (*V.O.*) What can I say? What can I add to this universal outpouring of lamentation, except, all of us who care so deeply should run right now to their neighborhood bookstore and purchase the book.

HARRY: Sandy!

(LORI *giggles.*)

MAN: (*V.O.*) And purchase it in the hardcover because that's the way Axel would've wanted it.

HARRY: I should've killed him instead.

MAN: (*V.O.*) In fact, why not express your grief by picking up the compelte set of seventeen books in the new, boxed edition, sure to become a collectors' item.

STREET ANNOUNCER: (*V.O.*) Thank you. We now return you to our—

MAN: (*V.O.*) And I hear they're coming out with memorial t-shirts and buttons and other moderately priced memorabilia.

STREET ANNOUNCER: (*V.O.*) Well, Sir, you seem to be quite knowledgeable. Might you be connected in some way?

MAN: (*V.O.*) No, no. I'm just a concerned citizen on his way to lunch.

(HARRY *shuts off the radio and turns to* LORI.)

HARRY: You read the new book?

LORI: (*Acknowledging the manuscript she holds.*) Yes.

HARRY: Oh.

(*They look at each other.*)

LORI: You watch the filming?

HARRY: Filming? That's what all of the noise is, outside?

LORI: Mmn. They shot the final scene just now. I thought I saw you standing at the window.

HARRY: Me? No, I might have passed by, maybe a quick look, so, how did it go?

LORI: Slowly. It took him a few takes, actually.

HARRY: (*Erupts*) Thirty seven! Thirty seven takes it took him to die! Thirty seven takes they got Moses through the Dead Sea, Ingrid Bergman out of Morocco, Dorothy back to Kansas, burned Atlanta—

LORI: Yeah but there were bullets, and knives flying all over the place.

HARRY: So what, knives. You want knives? Tony Perkins, Janet Leigh, five takes, tops. And that was in the shower naked. I could've killed him in the shower naked, but no, I want to be magnaminous. I wanted to give him a love scene. So, what does he do with it?

LORI: Listen, you can't really blame him.

HARRY: They're in the taxi, she takes his hand, very good. She places it gently upon her quivering breast, wonderful, terrific, just like I wrote.

LORI: She quivered very nicely.

HARRY: Lovely quivering, consummate actress. She tenderly brings him down on top of her, they're lying on the back seat together, beautiful, touching. Okay. Up come the bad guys. The camera dollies back. A bakers dozen of the KGB elite. Thirteen Russians, shooting and knifing. And shooting, sub-machine gun; Brakka Brakka Brakka! Right! And knifing, stilettos; Whistling, slicing through the air, Sssssss! Right! Now. Mademoiselle Yvette Bonsoir, who has rolled through a secret compartment, climbs out of the trunk and legs it down Lexington Avenue. Right? Wrong. Why? Because she is not in the trunk. Why? Because she is trapped in the arms of Justin Dean, who, with three hundred bullets and ten dozen stilettos in him, manages to lift his head up to the shattered windshield and scream . . . All right! I'll go! But I'm taking the bitch with me!

(*He looks at* LORI, *spent.*)

HARRY: Thirty six times.

LORI: Well, it was very traumatic for him.

HARRY: There is no such thing as traumatic license. It would have gone on forever except the director threatened to kill him in a hat.

(*He picks up the new manuscript and looks at it. He turns.*)

HARRY: Lori.

LORI: Dad. I read it very carefully.

HARRY: I know. I know you did. Because I know that you understand how important this is to me.

(LORI *shakes her head.*)

HARRY: Good. But listen, you mustn't let that get in the way of your honest opinion, because it's only your honest opinion that means anything to me.

(LORI *looks at him.*)

HARRY: I'm dedicating this book to you, you know.

(LORI *looks at him.*)

HARRY: Okay, go ahead!

(*He throws his arms around his head and hides his face.* SANDY *bursts into the room. He carries a briefcase.*)

SANDY: Brilliant! When I'm wrong, I'm wrong. Okay? Fine. Harry. Axel's worth twice as much dead than he was alive. You knew? I thought you were out of you mind but you're brilliant!

HARRY: (*Still hiding his face.*) No t-shirts, no buttons!

SANDY: What are you out of your mind? Look what I've got here. (*He opens the briefcase.*) Here's from the toy company. We got; for everybody with the Axel Troy Doll, The Axel Troy Doll Burial Kit. You know what you get? Dirt. Bag of dirt, twelve dollars. Slightly more for the deluxe model with perpetual care.

HARRY: No dirt.

SANDY: No dirt. Okay. Fine. There's lots more.

HARRY: No more.

SANDY: No more. (*Turns*) Lori. Hug me. You're the only reason I come here.

(LORI *hugs* SANDY. HARRY *looks through the briefcase.*)

HARRY: What's this?

SANDY: What?

HARRY: In here. There's a book in here.

SANDY: So?

HARRY: So, what are you doing with a book?

SANDY: Must have fallen in.

HARRY: (*Pulls out a paperback book.*) *Great Expectations.* (*Looks at* SANDY, *bewildered.*) A good book, too.

SANDY: Dickens. Because you're fond of him.

HARRY: Yes, I am. Since when are you?

SANDY: I tried to be, Harry. I thought if I knew what it was about this stuff that makes it literature and what attraction it holds for you, maybe I could understand you a little better.

HARRY: Sandy, I'm moved.

SANDY: Yeah? Don't be. (*Picks up the book.*) Because I don't care that his name is Pip, or how he got to be called Pip, or anything about him if you want to know. (*He turns to* LORI.) You care that his name is Pip?

LORI: That really doesn't have anything to do with anything, Sandy.

SANDY: Exactly the way I feel. Where'd you read this, college?

LORI: Mn hmn.

SANDY: Uh huh. In college I might've cared.

HARRY: You didn't go to college.

SANDY: So what? I do all right.

(HARRY *sighs.*)

SANDY: Besides, to have to have a college education in order to care for something is unnatural. Anyway, I tried to read it and that's enough.

HARRY: (*Looking through the book.*) Mmn. I see it's dog eared all the way to page one.

SANDY: Maybe I'm wrong, maybe I'm not so wrong, so, I submitted the book.

HARRY: *Great Expectations*? You submitted a classic?

SANDY: I had it typed up in manuscript form and sent it to three publishing houses. A brand new, untitled work, under the name Harry Leeby.

HARRY: Me?

SANDY: You wanted to write a good book? Now you did.

HARRY: What good does that do me?

SANDY: Not much. You were totally rejected.

HARRY: (*Startled*) What?

SANDY: (*Pulls three letters out of his briefcase and reads.*) Not suitable for our current needs, not suitable for our current needs, and—

HARRY: It's not current material.

SANDY: So? It's a period piece. Big sellers these days. Shouldn't they at least have seen potential?

HARRY: Yes.

SANDY: (*Waves the last letter.*) This last one does. (*Reads*) Although this is not what we are looking for at the moment, Mr. Leeby does show a degree of spark and I should like to meet with him at our mutual convenience.

HARRY: Culture at last.

SANDY: I thought so too, until I called to explain it was just a little experiment of mine, and the writer was really Charles Dickens.

HARRY: What did he say?

SANDY: He said he didn't care what your name was and you have an appointment, Thursday.

LORI: Congratulations, Dad.

SANDY: Don't waste your time. Guess what, Harry. It doesn't pay for you to be Dickens, after all.

HARRY: Why not?

SANDY: You outsell him. I did research. In its twenty-five years, the Duncan Foster catalogue has totally outsold the Charles Dickens catalogue. It has also outsold the Mark Twain catalogue, and the only reason they're even in your league is because they're taught in schools and if they taught Duncan Foster in schools instead maybe I would have gone to college and then where would you be?

HARRY: I'll be this month's featured selection in the *Literary Guild Magazine*!

(JUSTIN *enters. He wears slacks and a sweater and looks ten years older for not being* AXEL *anymore.*)

SANDY: Justin! Great news! You're worth twice as much, dead!

LORI: (*To* HARRY) Then, you should've stopped writing Axel after the first book.

HARRY: What?

SANDY: What?

JUSTIN: I've just stopped in to say goodbye.

ACT TWO

LORI: (*To her father*) Why did you write a second book if you already made enough money to do what you wanted?

SANDY: Enough money? I don't understand that. What does she mean?

JUSTIN: My work here would seem to be complete. I really must be getting back as soon as possible.

HARRY: I'm afraid that only works in retrospect, Lori. (*Points at* SANDY.) Because I had this guy over here who fixed it up so the first thing we did when we got rich was go bankrupt.

SANDY: I was young. I was wreckless.

JUSTIN: Didn't anybody want to know why I must be getting back as soon as possible?

HARRY: I used to visit Sandy in the mail room. He'd have me sorting mail while he told me all of the wonderful things he was going to do for me. We spent all our time sorting and dreaming.

JUSTIN: Offers! I've been deluged. As soon as word got out about my current availability!

SANDY: He dreamt of a Pulitzer Prize.

HARRY: He dreamt of a Rolls Royce.

JUSTIN: I have to choose between twenty, thirty projects.

HARRY: So he makes a wonderful deal on *My Gun Is My Jury*!

SANDY: I read that one!

HARRY: And we get our first check. Fifty thousand dollars!

SANDY: Five thousand dollars!

HARRY: With which he buys a Rolls Royce.

SANDY: I was young. I overextended.

LORI: How could you buy a Rolls Royce?

SANDY: Forty-eight monthly payments.

LORI: How long did you have it?

SANDY: One month.

HARRY: He used to make me drive him to the mail room in it. We'd wait on the corner until the big boys of the agency arrived and then he made me pull up. He got out of the back of the car, shook their hands, slapped them on the back and went inside. They fired him.

SANDY: It was worth every second.

HARRY: Mmn. He parlayed his first success into penury and unemployment. I could see what a shrewdie I had become involved with.

SANDY: And you did better? Mr. Young Entrepreneur? He hired a business manager. A turtle. Two hundred years old.

HARRY: He was great. I liked him because he talked slowly. Exactly as slowly as Sandy talks fast. I let him handle my money.

SANDY: He gave forty-five thousand dollars to a turtle!

HARRY: So, I've got my agent on one side of me, going . . .

SANDY: Buy a house! Buy a big house! Real estate. Something with a swimming pool. Terra firma. Tara. We'll never be hungry again!

LORI: (*To* SANDY) Why did you want him to buy a house?

SANDY: Because they repossessed mine.

HARRY: And I've got my business manager on the other side of me, going —

SANDY: (*Alarmed*) No. Harry!

HARRY: (*Agonizingly slow*) We will put this money into tax-free municipal bonds.

SANDY: (*Tortured*) Oh Harry, don't.

HARRY: (*Slower*) We will take fifteen thousand dollars and buy Cheektawaga Maryvale Union Free School District Bonds.

SANDY: (*Claps his hands to his ears.*) Harry, stop, this is brutal.

HARRY: (*Slower*) We will take the remaining twenty thousand dollars and purchase New Jersey Turnpike Revenue Bonds.

(SANDY *screams*)

Act Two

LORI: New Jersey Turnpike?

HARRY: He loved the turnpike. It was triple A rated.

LORI: Whatever happened to him?

SANDY: I killed him! I buried him in a lovely tree lined spot alongside the Secaucus toll plaza.

HARRY: I had to let him go. He did such a wonderful job that any money I made was completely protected by all of the money I made. I had four dollars. The rest I couldn't touch. He had nothing, I had four dollars.

LORI: So, what happened?

HARRY: What happened? The unthinkable happened. People loved the book. The first printing sold out in ten minutes. I was horrified. (*To* SANDY) You swore to me that wouldn't happen!

SANDY: I was young. I was wrong.

HARRY: (*To* LORI) People loved the book. They stopped me on the street to let me know. I tried to tell them they were making a mistake but they wouldn't listen. But this was very good because who was I writing for after all? So, I was resolved that as long as people loved the book, I would love to write more for them. (*To* SANDY) And because you told me it was only a novelty and would wear off.

SANDY: Wrong again.

HARRY: Second printing. Ten minutes! I was very nervous now. We were becoming a phenomenon, which was something I didn't want to do while I was alive. But it was out of my hands. My last chance was . . . (*Turns to* JUSTIN.) You. You were the cause of my first great conflict. In my heart I knew you were the worst choice in the world to play that role. But I also knew if there was anybody, any person alive in the world, who could single-handedly stem the public tide and make Axel repulsive, it was you! And you let me down and I hate you.

JUSTIN: Thank you.

HARRY: You're welcome.

(HARRY *sits, miserable.* JUSTIN *continues.*)

JUSTIN: Well, I'm sure you'll understand there isn't the time for long goodbyes. (*Turns to* LORI) Lori . . . Can it be so long ago I pushed you on the swings in Central Park? And watched the animals count off the hours on the Delacorte clock?

HARRY: You never did any of those things.

JUSTIN: (*Wheels on him*) You're killing the moment! (*Turns*) Sandy—

SANDY: Quick, Justin. Time is money.

JUSTIN: I just want to say that I have long been a fan of your business acumen and when the time comes for me to jot down my remembrances, I will certainly consider the use of your services.

SANDY: I appreciate that. If it means anything to you, I never read the books because they only ruin the movies for me.

JUSTIN: (*Hugs* SANDY) You dear man.

(JUSTIN *breaks from* SANDY, *moves to* HARRY, *and peers at him.*)

HARRY: Stop looking at me like I'm the Wizard of Oz. I have nothing more to give you.

JUSTIN: (*Solemn*) It's twenty-five years Duncan, and we are not friends. We never cared to find out anything about each other. Perhaps it would have been that much more worthwhile if we had. I only want you to know that if you chance to think of me in the future, I harbor no ill will in that you have taken away my reason for living. I brook no malevolence in that you have removed my purpose for getting up in the morning. And whatever your new book is I hope it dies! Oh, I feel so much better. (*He moves to the door.*)

HARRY: Why, Norman Frumpkin.

JUSTIN: Ahh!

HARRY: That was the first human sentiment I have ever heard you express!

JUSTIN: What?

SANDY: What?

Act Two

HARRY: I said—

JUSTIN: I heard what you said. To whom?

HARRY: I was attempting to reach Norman Frumpkin.

JUSTIN: Gahh!

HARRY: Is he in?

JUSTIN: Of course he's in! The clock's just struck twelve. I expect my limousine's been turned into a pumpkin, also.

SANDY: What? What are you talking about? Who's Norman Frumpkin? I want to know!

(HARRY *and* LORI *turn and look at* JUSTIN.)

JUSTIN: (*Purges*) I would have been third-generation shoe repair! My father, like his father before him, was Frumpkin's resoling of Flatbush Avenue—

SANDY: (*Incredulous*) Brooklyn?

JUSTIN: You know it??

(SANDY *holds up his shoe.* JUSTIN *recoils in horror.*)

JUSTIN: I was inevitably next unless I could devise some means of escape!

SANDY: Just a minute. Are you trying to tell me, that the entire world believes, that Axel Troy has been portrayed by Justin Dean from Britain—

JUSTIN: I was in my twenties and looking frighteningly convincing wearing my gray apron.

SANDY: When in fact he has been protrayed by a Norman Frumpkin from Brooklyn—

JUSTIN: And holding those tiny nails in my mouth.

SANDY: And that I am, in part, responsible for perpetuating a global misconception? (*He considers that.*) I love this business!

JUSTIN: I had read about a motion picture which was causing quite some excitement because it was being shot in Hoboken.

HARRY: (*Smiles*) *On the Waterfront.*

JUSTIN: Yes! And they were looking for . . . extras! So, I made my way to the wharves where I was given the address of a casting company in New York City. Well, the office was filled with aspirants, all looking very much like dock workers, which led the secretary to conclude I must have been there for the other film they were casting which, she informed me, was a British project and I said . . . (*Heavily accented*) . . . Umn, yas, as a matter of fact I'm just in from London. So, she buzzed her boss over the intercom and said, it's Justin from London, Which was how I got into the movies, ta da!

LORI: And how Norman Frumpkin got lòst in the shuffle?

JUSTIN: I figured he was safe in the old neighborhood and someday I'd come 'round to collect him.

SANDY: I am shocked!

JUSTIN: On the occasions I snuck back for a visit, my mother was so proud, she thought I was quite talented. Of course, my father would look at me, spit nine nails into a heel and say "*That's* talent, Mr. Secret Agent!"

SANDY: I am standing here, shocked!

JUSTIN: Naturally, with each visit I found I had lost a bit more feeling for the place. I haven't returned in some time.

SANDY: All those years we might have palled around!

JUSTIN: (*Turns to* SANDY) Why? You were raised on Flatbush Avenue?

SANDY: No, Stratford on Avon. Of course Flatbush Avenue! Justin, you fooled me! I can spot a Brooklyn boy across the room but you I never would've guessed. You've completely lost it!

JUSTIN: What do you mean, lost it? This is just an act. A facade. Underneath, I'm as Brooklyn as you are.

SANDY: What are you, crazy? Just because you're born there you think you're entitled?

JUSTIN: What?

ACT TWO   55

SANDY: You have to keep going back! You have to stay one with the community.

JUSTIN: What?

SANDY: When's the last time you ate a piece of cheesecake at Junior's?

JUSTIN: Well, I . . .

SANDY: Forget it. You're gone.

(JUSTIN *hangs his head.*)

HARRY: You're better off. You need to be Justin Dean for all of those movie offers anyway.

JUSTIN: Oh, yes, well, actually there aren't as many as all that. You see, it seems I've done such a good job becoming Axel, no one thinks I can become much anything else, right now, you see. So, it would be of some small comfort to know there was still a Norman Frumpkin to whom I might return.

HARRY: Sandy, he's reaching out. Isn't there something you can do?

SANDY: No.

HARRY: Justin, it's going to be hard after twenty-five years but you're going to have to remember how to speak normally.

JUSTIN: I am speaking normally.

HARRY: No. Norman normally.

SANDY: Let me hear you say Erasmus High School.

JUSTIN: Erasmus High School.

SANDY: Prospect Park.

JUSTIN: Prospect Park.

SANDY: I am shocked.

JUSTIN: No! I can do it. Listen (*Impassioned*) Brighton Beach!

(*The telephone rings.* HARRY *picks it up.*)

SANDY: I don't know Justin, it's more than talking, it's an attitude.

HARRY: (*Into the phone*) Hello?

SANDY: It's not Cinzano, it's egg cream.

HARRY: (*Into the phone*) Oh hello, Garfield, how are you?

SANDY: (*Yells to the phone*) If that's my shyster borther I'm not here. I haven't heard from him in weeks. He must want something.

HARRY: (*Into the phone*) Hold on. I'll tell him.

SANDY: What? Tell me. I want to know:

HARRY: Your mother misses you. Garfield wants you to come to dinner.

SANDY: (*Suspiciously*) He wants me to come to dinner? What does he mean by that?

HARRY: He means dinner. You know. Lunch at night.

SANDY: (*Into the phone*) Four Seasons, my table, you pick up the check, those are my terms. No I don't want to hear a counter offer. Le Cirque, your table, we split the check? Only if you pick up lunch next time at the Tea Room. Absolutely, that's a deal breaker . . .

(JUSTIN *discovers the Axel Troy burial kit, holds it up, and sighs pathetically.* SANDY *looks at* JUSTIN, *sympathetically.*)

SANDY: (*Into the phone*) Garfield, how's this? I'll pick up the check, we sit anywhere you want, I just want to pick the place. Fine. I want to go to Nathan's.

(JUSTIN *looks up.*)

SANDY: (*Into the phone*) Yeah, you heard me right. Nathan's Famous. The one in the old neighborhood.

(JUSTIN *looks at* SANDY.)

SANDY: (*Into the phone*) And Garfield, I'm bringing a friend.

(*He hangs up the phone.* JUSTIN *moves to him.*)

ACT TWO 57

JUSTIN: (*Bursting*) That's swell! That's swell of you, Sandy! Thank you.

SANDY: Good. (*Smiles*) We'll ride the Cyclone. You got a car waiting outside?

JUSTIN: Yes.

SANDY: Sit in it. I've got two minutes of business with Mr. Spykiller.

(JUSTIN *turns to* HARRY)

JUSTIN: Umm, Harry—

HARRY: No, Justin, don't say anything kind to me. I still hate you and if you take that away from me I don't know what I'll do.

JUSTIN: I just wanted to say that I know you've never agreed with my interpretation of your character but you should also know I always did the best I could do.

HARRY: Well, I don't think anyone else could have cared so much.

JUSTIN: That's because I've always believed it was great stuff!

(*He turns and heads for the door.*)

LORI: Justin.

(*He stops and turns to her. She applauds him. He bows to her, and exits.*)

(SANDY *pulls one more contract from his briefcase. He puts it in front of* HARRY *and hands him a pen.*)

HARRY: What?

SANDY: Sign.

HARRY: What is it?

SANDY: Three hundred thousand dollars.

HARRY: For what?

SANDY: For what. That's what they want to know. For whatever it is.

HARRY: My new book?

SANDY: Yeah.

HARRY: For whatever it is?

SANDY: Look, it's the best I can do without them seeing it.

HARRY: So, why don't we let them see it?

SANDY: Sign.

(HARRY *signs the contract.* SANDY *puts it back into the briefcase. He notices the manuscript on the desk.*)

SANDY: This it?

HARRY: Yes.

SANDY: (*Picks up the manuscript and reads the title.*) Demons (*He turns to* HARRY.) Still on that, huh?

HARRY: Yes.

SANDY: So, when can you give it to me?

HARRY: I just want to look it over once more.

SANDY: (*To* LORI) You read it?

LORI: Uh huh.

SANDY: What did you think?

HARRY: I was just about to find out before I was besieged.

SANDY: Okay, I'm leaving. Harry, now that you're going to be just another classic novelist, you think you might be able to talk to me when I call you?

HARRY: You think you might be able to read my classic novels when I give them to you?

SANDY: No deal! I'm very busy catching up on important reading, lately.

HARRY: Prospective clients?

SANDY: Nope. All of yours I missed.

HARRY: Oh.

SANDY: I just want to see what all of the fuss is about.

ACT TWO 59

HARRY: How do you like them?

SANDY: I'll tell you Harry, they're good.

HARRY: You think so?

SANDY: Yeah, no kidding.

(*They look at each other.*)

SANDY: You have a gift from God, Kiddo, and I encourage it. That's what I do. I don't have to read it to recognize it and believe in it, and I do. I always have. And a world full of people back me up and make me right. So, it's times like these when I realize we're as famous as Nathan's that I have to go there and eat a hot dog or else I'll lose my whole perspective and end up conceited. You know what I'm talking about?

HARRY: Yes. You eat a hot dog. I sleep on the floor.

SANDY: To each his own. (*Turns*) Lori. Hug me. You're the only reason I come here.

(*They hug each other.* SANDY *exits.* LORI *Shuts the door, turns to her father, and looks at him.*)

HARRY: Where were we?

LORI: Well, you were like this.

(LORI *throws her arms around her head, hiding her face.*)

HARRY: Oh yeah. (*He sits on his desk. He puts his arms back around his head.*)

(LORI *picks up the manuscript.*)

LORI: We had that white spinet piano. I was six years old before I was tall enough to discover it wasn't just furniture. You ran from your typewriter to see what all of the noise was and saw me having such a good time banging on the keys, you thought I might be musically inclined. So ten years of lessons for me! After which, I knew what the notes were, and I knew theory, but I was playing with far less feeling. I knew you wanted me to be talented, and I wanted to be talented for you, but I wasn't. I'm not. Except now, what moves me most, is piano music. What's so strong in me is the appreciation.

HARRY: I spent three months, day and night, working on this book.

LORI: When you told me I didn't have to take piano lessons anymore, I wasn't as crushed as you thought.

HARRY: The most wretched, tortuous, ninety days and nights of my time on Earth.

LORI: I was relieved. And not just a little relieved. It was the greatest relief of my life.

HARRY: (*Considers the manuscript.*) And the fruit of my first decent suffering . . . is rotten. How is that possible?

LORI: Not to be talented meant I could play with my friends!

HARRY: I hate words! I hate sentences! Lori! Save me! Maybe you like my book! Who am I to stand in judgment? I have no objectivity. Only you do. You're the public. You're the world!

LORI: Dad, your book is rotten.

HARRY: It's a cruel world.

LORI: And not just a little rotten. If it means anything to you, among the rotten books, this one's classic!

HARRY: (*Looks at* LORI.) Thank you, Lori. Perhaps you're hiding some other rays of sunshine you'd care to point my way.

LORI: (*Smiles*) Just that I know you agree with me, which makes it unnecessary for me to have to drag you to your old hometown and feed you hot dogs until you recognize who you really are.

HARRY: I'm fifty-one years old and I know who I am. And I know I have done a remarkable thing in my life. I have created one unique and important character for whose presence the world is a better place. (*He turns to* LORI.) Could she give me a hug? (*They hold each other.*)

LORI: Stephen asked me to marry him.

HARRY: Lori. Just because you don't like something I've done doesn't mean you have to leave forever!

LORI: I'm not leaving. Marriage would never stand in the way of my job as Executive Daughter.

ACT TWO

HARRY: I don't know. This is going to take a lot of waffles.

LORI: Every morning. Right before we go to work.

HARRY: Work on what?

LORI: On whatever you care to imagine.

HARRY: (*Looks at her.*) I do care to imagine. (*He picks up the manuscript.*)

LORI: What are you going to do with it?

HARRY: I'm going to put it where it belongs. (*He moves to his library.*) Right next to *Huckleberry Finn* (*He puts the manuscript on a shelf.*) . . . who said at the end of his adventures—There ain't nothing more to write about, and I am rotten glad of it, because if I'd a knowed what a trouble it was to make a book I wouldn't a tackled it, and ain't a going to no more.

(*He sits on the library ladder.* LORI *watches him.*)

HARRY: I just want to sit here.

(LORI *turns to leave.*)

HARRY: Where are you going?

LORI: Stephen. He's real, he's alive, and I want to tell him yes before Sandy gets him a better offer! (*She stops at the door.*) I don't have to worry about you being alone?

HARRY: I'm not alone.

(*She looks at him and smiles. She exits.*)

(HARRY *sits a moment and then steps off the ladder. He moves to a desk drawer by the manual typewriter. He opens it and removes a key. He unlocks another drawer underneath and pulls it open. He takes out a hat and holds it in his hands.*)

HARRY: So? I've heard from everybody except you. It is your funeral. Guest of honor. Final speaker. Some last words maybe? (*He puts the hat on his head.*) Yeah. I got something to say. I say, we ate a lot of steak, we killed a lot of guys. Who got treated better? Come on. It's been swell. Forget it.

(*He takes the hat off his head and holds it. He looks over the books between the bookends. He pulls one out and flips through the pages. He puts the hat back on his head.*)

HARRY: Yeah. Monte Carlo. Me at the table with all of the high rollers and my dice said, seven, eleven. You did that for me, didn't you? Hey, you're a real guy, I always thought so. Done is done, what are you worried about? (*He takes the hat off and puts it down. He chuckles to himself. He tries to avoid the hat. He puts it back on his head.*) Yeah. We've been all over. Sleeping late in the morning, out by the pool in the afternoon sun, and in the evening, make some love, kill some guys, not a bad existence and I'm appreciative. And not for one second did I wonder who it was pulling me out of the tight spots. Don't get me wrong, I'm good. I'm the best there is but it was you behind me pal, and I always knew it. I'll tell you something though, a confession. That little incident in the Arctic, buried under the ice avalanche. I thought I was in trouble that time. I had fear there. Who could have guessed that directly below me was the subterranean headquarters of the Eskimo underworld, and as the ground split open I was sucked down, not to a frozen death, but right into the middle of a prisoner interrogation room where who should be chained, absolutely naked to a wall, but a quivering Mademoiselle Yvette Bonsoir. And how did I take advantage of this fortuitous turn of events? I moved toward her, unzipped my parka, and put it around her shoulders as I freed her from bondage. I bring this up only because it occurred to me as I lay in the back of the taxi in my ventillated state, that I have not exactly been repaid in kind. Now, I realize you've needed time to put things in perspective lately and to decide what is important and what is not and whatever you've chosen, good luck pal, far be it from me to question you wisdom. (*He grabs the hat from his head and immediately puts it back.*) Which, in our twenty-five year association, did I ever ask you a question? Did I ask you a question on the ocean floor when they severed my oxygen line? Did I ask you a question in free fall when they shredded my parachute? Did I ask you a question in Venice when they firebombed the gondola? Not a question! No question! Well, it may come as quite a shock to you buddy, but my first inclination was not to free her from any bondage. And while you've been busy considering what is important and what is not, I've been busy talking to your Mr. Dickens and

Mr. Twain because they happened to be the first dead people I ran into and you want to know what they think is important? That she is out there. The thing that is really important is that she could do this to me and she is out there somewhere and now I have a question! And my question is . . . What are we going to do about it?

(*He stops. He pushes the hat to the back of his head and stands still. Gradually, he smiles. He turns to his manual typewriter, takes the cover off it and carefully folds it. He puts it back into the drawer. He wheels his chair away from the electric typewriter, to the manual typewriter, and sits. He takes a piece of typing paper and loads the typewriter. He types effortlessly. He stops and reads.*)

HARRY: Axel Troy sat up in his coffin and straightened his tie. He had unfinished business with a certain French woman.

(*Satisfied, he resumes typing, as the lights fade out, and the curtain falls.*)

THE END

www.ingramcontent.com/pod-product-compliance
Lightning Source LLC
Chambersburg PA
CBHW060218050426
42446CB00013B/3102